ARCHITECT

© 2024 Julie Dascoli

All rights reserved. No part of this book may be reproduced or transmitted in any form or by any means, electronic or mechanical, including photocopying, recording or by any information storage and retrieval system, without prior permission in writing from the publisher.

Published in 2024 by Amba Press, Melbourne, Australia.
www.ambapress.com.au

Previously published in 2015 by Hawker Brownlow Education.
This edition replaces all previous editions.

ISBN: 9781923116948 (pbk)
ISBN: 9781923116955 (ebk)

A catalogue record for this book is available from the National Library of Australia.

ARCHITECT

Written by Julie Dascoli

Photography by Laura Dascoli

Dear Reader,

Welcome to this volume of the *Real People Real Careers* series. I hope you'll enjoy learning about another exciting job people can do.

Before you read on, I'd like to say a few thank-yous to the people who helped to make this book possible.

Firstly, thank you to Laura Dascoli, who took the photographs you see in the book, and to Donna Dascoli, who provided initial editing and computer support services.

Secondly, my thanks to the staff and students in Years 4, 5 and 6 of the Mossgiel Park Primary School class of 2016 for their unwavering help and support.

And finally, I'm doubly grateful to Gerard, who generously gave up his time to help others learn about his profession – and to show them all the ways in which his job rules!

Happy reading!

Julie Dascoli

ARCHITECT

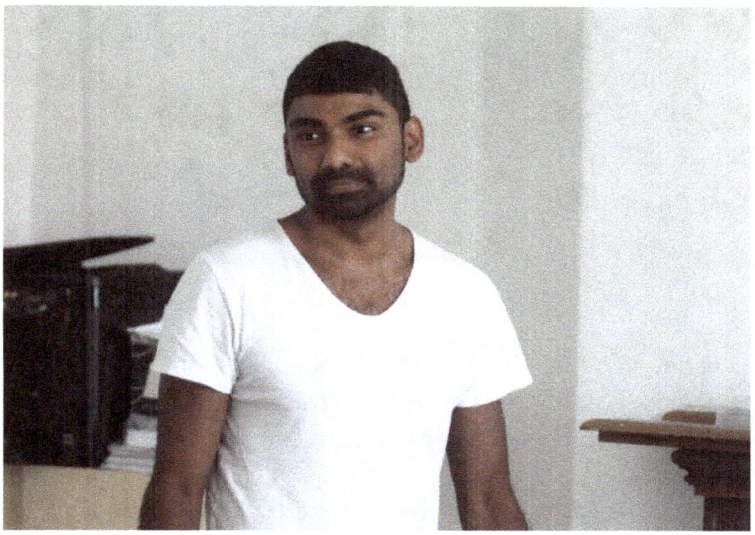

My name is Gerard and I am an Architect. I began primary school in my birth country of Sri Lanka.

I enjoyed school very much, but when I completed year four I moved to Australia with my family as my father took a job opportunity as a Doctor in a large country town.

It was very scary moving to another country and a new school, but once we got there it was great. I made new friends and settled in to a different way of life. I was in year five at this time.

I continued on to a local state secondary school. When I was in year nine my father was once again **transferred,** this time closer to the city. I completed years ten, eleven and twelve here.

All through secondary school I imagined I wanted to be a doctor so I chose subjects accordingly, such as **Physics,** Maths and **Chemistry.** I also learned piano privately as my mother is an **acclaimed** piano teacher and it was a lovely distraction from science topics.

On completion of year twelve it was time to apply for **university** courses. I applied for the **Bachelor of Medicine** at all of the universities that offered it, and was delighted when I was accepted at my first choice.

I was only in the course for three weeks and I was miserable. I couldn't take another day so decided to change courses.

I was able to transfer to another course, and this time I began a Bachelor of Planning and Design.

I completed this course, but to be honest I did not really enjoy it either. I didn't know what I was going to do. I decided to take a break and go to England.

While I was there I worked as a waiter in a bar. I knew that this wasn't a career for me, that I was just filling in time. It was not **stimulating** enough and I did not earn enough money to advance myself.

I continued to look for jobs and eventually I found one working for an **architectural firm**.

Now I knew what I wanted to do. This job was so exciting. The firm was working on two major airports, huge shopping centres, **ports** and all kinds of very interesting jobs.

I then knew that I needed to go home to Australia and do a Bachelor of Architecture. This took me another three years, but it was worth it.

I then I did a **Master's** of Architecture.

While I was doing my last few years of university I began teaching architecture and doing a few jobs for friends and other contacts. I designed **company logos** and I had the opportunity to design a café for a friend of mine. He did not have much money so I made a lot of the things we needed myself. When a local shopping centre saw my work they started giving me a lot of work as well.

Shortly after this I began my own architecture business. The work was trickling in by **word of mouth**. I designed many buildings, including some prominent ones in and around the city.

About this time, I was looking everywhere for a particular light for a job. I owned one of these lights in my office. I looked high and low and eventually found the creator. His name is Alex. He made the lights for my job. They looked amazing. We worked together so well we decided to go into business together. We continue to work together designing and **manufacturing** lighting and furniture. Our pieces are sought after all over the world. At the same time, I continue to run my Architecture business. This keeps me very busy, but it is very satisfying.

Colour charts

Tasks I perform every day

- → The first job I do when I arrive at work is checking my emails, as this **communication** is often from **clients** that need some information. Alternatively, they can be from suppliers with problems that need addressing or staff with queries. These are issues that I need to know about immediately.

- → I have a daily meeting with the staff at the workshop to discuss issues there.

- → I also have a daily meeting with the staff at the architecture office. These meetings help with the daily running of these businesses and ensure that any issues are dealt with swiftly and success stories are shared straight away.

- → I meet with any clients to update or find out further information about their needs for their job.

- → I work at my computer, as this is where most of the designing is done.

- → Later I work at the **workshop** designing parts for future products.

- → I follow up on any outstanding **invoices** and other paperwork.

ARCHITECT PAGE 9

Interesting facts about my job

- → You can be an architect without being a designer, I just happen to have chosen to do both.

- → I can work from anywhere in the world. An example of this is: One time I was in Morocco, my client was in Vietnam, while I was designing a restaurant in Brisbane and my office was in Melbourne. We were able to have a four-way conversation.

- → I can take long holidays and still keep an eye on what's happening in the office via modern technology.

- → I can sometimes finish work at four o'clock and sometimes I am still at the office at ten o'clock in the evening.

- → At any given time I could average 10 Architecture clients and 20 lighting or furniture clients.

- → Lunchtime varies: it could be a sandwich on the run or a few hours at a café with clients to discuss their job needs.

- → I have designed many things, from whole buildings to furniture and teapots.

What I wear to work

I don't need to wear a uniform to work, but I do need to wear smart, professional dress.

When I go on building sites I need to wear protective clothing in **compliance** with building site **safety regulations.** This includes a **high-visibility** vest and **hard-hat**, like on the previous page.

> I don't need to wear a uniform to work, but I do need to wear smart, professional dress.

ARCHITECT

You could do my job if you:

- → enjoy working with people
- → are creative
- → can work in a team setting
- → enjoy making things
- → are a problem solver
- → are a good communicator
- → have a good imagination

Choosing carpet colours for a job

Samples to choose colours and textures

Plans

ARCHITECT

Related occupations

- → Draughtsman
- → Graphic designer
- → Landscape designer
- → Engineer
- → Surveyor

Various tools and equipment around the workshop

Gerard continues to operate his architecture and lighting/furniture businesses. He also still lectures at university. His hard work has paid off, as this is his dream job.

Glossary

Acclaimed — To speak highly of or be highly regarded. *Gerard's mother is an acclaimed piano teacher.*

Architectural firm — A company where buildings and other structures are designed. *Gerard enjoyed working for the Architectural firm in England.*

Bachelor of Medicine — The course that one does to become a doctor. *Gerard began a bachelor of medicine but quickly decided that he did not like it.*

Chemistry — The branch of science that studies the composition, structure and change of matter. *Gerard studied chemistry at high school.*

Clients — The collective name for a customer who pays a professional for their services. *Gerard has many clients in both of his businesses.*

Communication — The sharing of information by talking, emailing, texting or some other form. *Gerard has regular meetings to maintain good communication with his clients and staff.*

Company logo	A recognisable graphic design or symbol that identifies a company. *Gerard designed some company logos while he was studying.*
Compliance	The act of obeying wishes, requests or rules. *When entering a building site Gerard wears protective clothing in compliance with safety regulations.*
Hard-hat	A rigid protective helmet worn by workers in a construction, factory or roadside setting. *Gerard must wear a Hard-hat in line with building site regulations.*
High-visibility vest	Also known as a 'high-vis vest'. A vest that is worn over regular clothes to be more visible in a construction, factory or roadside setting. *Gerard must wear a high-vis vest in line with building-site regulations.*
Invoices	A document that informs a client what they have ordered, how much it's going to cost and what date they purchased it. *Sending and receiving invoices is a part of the office work that Gerard does regularly.*

Manufacturing — The process of making or building things. *Gerard and his business partner, Alex, manufacture lighting and furniture.*

Masters — An advanced university course in a specific area one can do after a degree. *Gerard completed a Master's degree to advance his qualifications.*

Physics — The natural science involving the study of matter, its motion through time and space, and related concepts like energy and force. *Physics is one of the science subjects Gerard studied at high school.*

Ports — A place on a waterway where ships can be loaded and unloaded. *When Gerard was in England he helped design ports, among other things.*

Safety regulations — The rules and laws put in place to protect people. *Gerard always follows safety regulations.*

Stimulating — To be interesting enough to keep one interested. *Gerard found that being a bar waiter was not stimulating for him.*

Transferred	To be moved from one place to another. *Gerard's father was transferred to different parts of the world, including Australia, for his job.*
University	A tertiary facility where students go to obtain a degree. *Gerard completed two university degrees.*
Word of mouth	Spreading information around from person to person, by talking. *Word of Gerard's work spread by word of mouth.*
Workshop	The place/factory where things get manufactured. *The furniture and lighting that Alex and Gerard make are made in the workshop.*

Other titles in this series

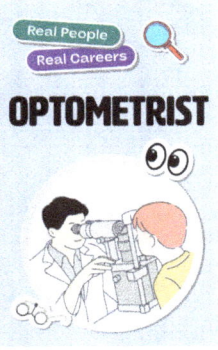

www.ingramcontent.com/pod-product-compliance
Lightning Source LLC
Chambersburg PA
CBHW070343120526
44590CB00017B/2994